POWERFUL PEOPLE

Handle
with
care!

ROSIE McCORMICK

Belitha Press

First published in the UK in 2002 by

Belitha Press Limited
A member of **Chrysalis** Books plc
64 Brewery Road, London N7 9NT

Copyright © Belitha Press Limited 2002
Text by Rosie McCormick

Editor: Kate Phelps
Designer: Peter Clayman
Illustrator: Woody
Consultant: Kathleen Robertson

ISBN 1 84138 430 5

British Library Cataloguing in Publication Data for this
book is available from the British Library.

Printed in Italy by Eurolitho S.p.A.

Some of the more unfamiliar words used in this book
are explained in the glossary on pages 46 and 47.

CONTENTS

Dear Reader

I expect your days and weeks are packed full of things to do like going to school, extra activities, hobbies – and, of course, lots of playing. Most of the time, you are probably busy doing something even when it's raining and you are complaining loudly that you have NOTHING to do. But as these days and weeks become years, do you ever stop to think about who you are or the person you are becoming? I expect not. It's more that you find your self loving something you used to hate like getting your hair cut or having a bath. Or hating something you used to love like playing hide-and-seek with a younger brother or sister. From the time you are a tiny baby until you become an adult, you are constantly growing and changing. You are growing up. Quite often these growing up years can seem like a roller coaster ride.

Roller coaster of life

Certain things can get you down like feeling shy, feeling like you don't fit in or struggling a little with school work. But then there are the times when life just seems like one big, fun-filled adventure. So as you make your way on this bumpy journey into adulthood take a moment once in a while to have a good look at the person you call you. Do you see anyone you recognize?

4

INTRODUCTION

Right about now, you are beginning to develop strong ideas about the things you like and don't like. You know you like chicken nuggets and cartoons, and you're certain you don't like cabbage, spinach and homework. You know who you enjoy playing with and who your favourite teachers are. So life's fairly straightforward. Or is it?

Don't worry – it's okay to admit that there are times when you just don't know what you like, want or feel. And your feelings can and do get the better of you. The fact is that you are experiencing lots of new things for the first time and aren't sure how to act. You are developing as a person but you don't quite know who that person is.

The thing to remember is that most, if not all, of the people your age are experiencing similar things. (Just bear that in mind when next you feel like screaming at your best friend.) And, for those rainy days, the following pages are full of tips and advice that might come in handy when facing some of life's more uncertain moments.

It's going to take some time for you to get to know just who you are or, more importantly, who you are becoming. So it's certainly going to take others even longer.

I'M ME

This won't stop family members and close friends who think they know you REALLY well from giving you lots and lots of advice about what to wear or do or say. Advice can be helpful so listen and store it for future use. Sometimes, though, too much advice can be frustrating, especially when you haven't figured out what YOU want to wear, do or say.

DON'T PANIC

As time goes by you will begin to develop strong views about the things you like and dislike. Certain activities or hobbies will interest you while others won't. You will begin to feel strongly about certain issues such as the environment or animal welfare. You will begin to identify the things that seem just right for you. The more confident you become and the more willing you are to let people know what you like, need or believe in, then the more they will actually get to know you. And this process never stops. Throughout your life you will continue to change and grow.

TOP TIP
Remember that your actions can tell others what kind of person you are.

EXPRESS YOURSELF

There are all kinds of ways you can, and I expect do, express yourself. Believe it or not, if you like playing football every minute of every day that tells people a little bit about who you are. It tells them that you are probably quite fit, that you are sure to have a favourite football team and player, and that you enjoy team sports. On the other hand, if you enjoy things like drama, debating and have lots to say in class, the chances are you're not shy, you're rather confident and, when you get a chance, you quite like an audience. Whether you enjoy sports, computers, drama, arts such as painting or sculpting, writing, fashion, science or whatever, your actions let others know a little bit about who you are.

I love greater spotted wombats

WHAT DO I LIKE?

There's only one way to find out if something suits you and that's to have a go. You might think that joining the cross-country team is a great idea – after all your best friend loves it. But if you discover that you hate running through muddy fields in the middle of winter, don't despair. It certainly doesn't mean that you are a failure or that you don't fit in. It simply means that a particular activity was not for you. Something else – preferably indoors where it's warm – may suit you better. It's worth trying things more than once, though, just to make sure that it is/isn't for you.

TOP TIP
Take the time to find out what things interest and suit you best.

'Maybe I'll try basket-weaving'

DON'T GIVE UP

From time to time most people doubt themselves and their abilities. If we discover that we're not particularly good at one thing, then we immediately tell ourselves that we are rubbish at everything. But of course this isn't true. The reality is that we can't be brilliant at every single thing we do. (Although occasionally there is someone around who is and they can be extremely annoying!)

I CAN DO THAT

The thing to remember is to try to have a positive attitude. Don't be scared if you don't understand something or think you can't do something well. Just be honest and explain how you are feeling. For example, if you feel that you struggle with maths or science, tell your parents and your teachers. As soon as they know about your concerns, they will help you get to grips with them. You may never become a maths or science super-brain. But that's because you're not meant to be. You might instead be a talented artist or sports person. Undoubtedly you have many strengths and some weaknesses. They all fit together to make you the person you are – and that's the way it's supposed to be.

'I don't think my talents lie in maths!'

TOP TIP
Be honest about the things you find difficult or don't like. Try your best and then relax.

Teacher: 'Simon, if two and two make four, what do four and four make?'
Simon: 'Typical! You answer the easy question and ask me the hard one!'

ACE ACHIEVEMENTS

If someone were to ask you, could you tell them what your best achievements are or what makes you most proud about being you? It could be anything – you've finally managed to climb the tallest tree in your garden, you've mastered your nine-times tables or that you were the one who found a neighbour's lost kitten.

'Nine nines are 81'

'Cor!'

'My cat!'

TOP TIP
Be proud of who you are and all the things you can do.

WELL DONE!

Don't forget to give yourself a big pat on the back from time to time. There are so many new experiences and challenges whizzing in and out of your world that you might forget just how well you are doing or just how much you have grown and developed in the past few months or years. Have pride in what you have achieved. Maybe think about all the things a friend has achieved and give them a pat on the back too.

FEELING SHY

A lot of people don't like being in the spotlight. They panic when they realize that all eyes are on them. They blush, sweat or forget what they wanted to say. This is a perfectly normal reaction. However some people do seem to manage the pressure of these kinds of situations a little better than others. If you are someone who stumbles, trips and turns bright red when asked to stand up in class and tell people a little bit about yourself, then these suggestions are especially for you.

AND ACTION!

• Take a deep breath. (Deep breaths help you to relax.)
• Speak slowly; try not to rush through what you have to say. If you rush, you are more likely to stumble over your words.
• Focus on a friendly face and imagine that you are simply talking to that person and not to the entire class.
• Try to smile and look relaxed (even though you're not). This will help your audience enjoy listening to you.
• Always remember that most people in this situation feel nervous and unsure too.

MAKING FRIENDS

Quite often, the things you are interested in or like doing draw you towards others. If you like music, you might belong to a musical group or play in a school band. If you like chess, you might belong to the school chess club. Mostly though, you make friends with people simply because you get along with them and enjoy playing with them.

DO I FIT IN?

But from time to time something can happen to make you feel like you don't fit in. A new person can join your circle of friends and that can change things. Your closest friend can move and suddenly you start to feel like you are on your own. Or you think you are the only one struggling with a topic at school. Feeling like you don't belong or fit in can be scary. However, what you need to realize is that it's not that you don't fit in, it's simply that something has happened to change the way things used to be. It's a new experience and you need to learn how to cope with it.

TALK IT OUT

The best way to tackle any situation that you don't fully understand or that makes you feel unhappy is to talk to someone about it. Parents, teachers and friends are there to listen and advise. Often they will help you see things a little more clearly and that way you can find a solution to the problem.

These challenges are all part of growing up and gaining experience about life. It's just a matter of figuring out what to do. Try to choose a good time for talking, though. Don't approach your teacher in the middle of lessons or your dad while he's trying to get ready for work.

'DAD!'

FABULOUS FRIENDS

Friends, as you already know, are very important. They are a big part of your life and always will be – even when you are all grown up. You choose your friends because you love being with them, because they are fun, because you have things in common and because you can talk to them. However, there are also times when you fall out or disagree with them. When this happens it can seem like the end of the world. But good friends usually work things out.

TOP TIP
If you and a friend have a problem, it's important to let each other know how you are feeling. Remember, listening is part of communicating as well.

'I hate you!'

'I hate you!'

STAYING FRIENDS

1 Always listen to what the other person has to say.
2 Try to understand their opinions and their feelings.
3 When you make a mistake, accept it and try to make amends.
4 Show how much you care by saying sorry.

IT'S A GOAL!
There are probably millions and zillions of things you want to achieve – like getting ten out of ten for the next spelling test, learning another language, receiving a gold star for a special history topic, playing football or netball for your school, learning to swim, juggle, roller-skate or walk on stilts! Whatever your ambitions, there are ways to achieve them:

TOP TIP
Achieving things often means a little bit of extra effort and thought.

❶ Think about or make a list of the things you hope to achieve.
❷ For each goal, figure out what you need to do to succeed. (For example, passing a test may require a little extra studying. Playing a sport well usually needs lots and lots of practice.)
❸ Set aside enough time to do these things.
❹ Talk to people who have already achieved these goals.
❺ Be patient – things don't always happen as quickly as we would like.
❻ Always remember that taking part and trying your best is what really matters.

THE FUTURE

You may not realize it now but your hobbies, interests and favourite subjects are already leading you towards your future. The things you enjoy and are interested in will help you to figure out a career path and a way to contribute to society when you are older. You can find out lots of information about careers, such as what qualifications, skills and training are needed, by reading books and asking questions. And, when you are older, you will probably receive careers advice from professionals. So don't worry, when the time comes you won't be expected to pick a career out of a hat and then you're stuck with it. The world is full of lots of opportunities just waiting for you!

Llama farmer

TOP TIP
Remember that you possess many skills and talents. You will discover many opportunities for you to fulfil your potential.

I'm very good with poodles!

CAREERS

'I can leap tall buildings!'

Mum: 'Mary, how was your first day of school? Did you learn lots and lots of things?'
Mary: 'I don't think so because my teacher wants me to come back again'.

CAREER TREE

Use the career tree to help you decide what career you might want to try. The branches tell you what subjects you like and the leaves give you possible career choices.

Theatre, TV, radio, film, education, advertising, publishing and design.

Industry, manufacturing, finance, medicine or teaching.

Computer manufacturing, programming, problem solving and software development.

Social work, health and medicine, the environment, animal welfare and law enforcement.

Professional sports person, coach, teacher, sport's journalist.

Computers and software

Art, drama and music

Maths and science

PSHE

Sports and PE

CAREER TREE

Money Matters

Money isn't the most important thing in life but it would be difficult to manage without it. The jobs that people do provide them with money. It pays for all the things we need in life such as homes, food, clothes, cars, holidays, telephones and TVs – and all your toys and games too.

The adults in your life have to manage the money they earn so that there is enough to pay for the important or essential things you and your family need. Sometimes this can mean that you don't get that new bike or scooter you were hoping for. Instead, the money is needed to fix the family car or pay an extra bill.

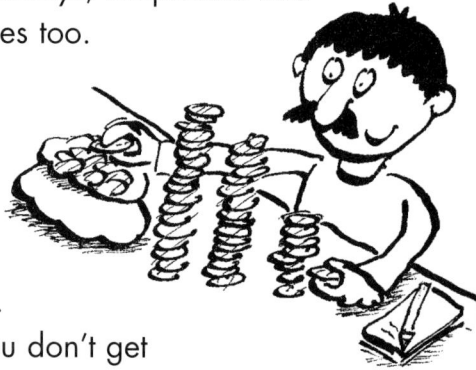

Handling Money

Just like the grown-ups, you need to learn how to handle money too. If, for example, you get pocket money on a Friday evening and by Saturday morning it's all gone, then perhaps you need to learn how to save a little. Make an effort to put some money aside for something you really want to buy rather than always relying on mum, dad and other relatives to get it for you. Start saving for special occasions like holidays and family birthdays. This way you will have money to spend when you really need some. Maybe think about opening a bank account or savings account where your money will earn interest.

> **TOP TIP**
> Learn to save and budget your pocket money or gift money. This will help you when you are older to manage larger amounts of money.

WHY SHOULD I CARE?

It's important that we all pay attention to the things that are happening in our world. We all live together on Planet Earth sharing its air, water and land. It's important to control pollution and waste disposal and care for wildlife. It's also essential that all people have enough food to eat, a safe place to live, an education and medical care. We have a responsibility to look after each other. If we think about how we live our lives on a daily basis, we can help to solve all kinds of problems. We can encourage everyone we know to recycle, to walk instead of drive and to save energy and water as much as possible. When bad things happen to people we can find out the facts and speak out. If we all work together, then we can build a brighter future for everyone.

Bob: 'When I grow up I want to be a millionaire. I'll buy an enormous house with no bathrooms in it.'
Tom: 'Why no bathrooms?'
Bob: 'Because I want to be filthy rich!'

Handle with care!

QUIZ TIME

Here's a little test to see how you handle some tricky situations.

1 Ever since a new friend joined your group of 'best' friends, things have not been the same. You are starting to feel left out. What should you do?
a) Talk it over and explain how you are feeling.
b) Ask the new friend to go away and leave 'your' friends alone.
c) Abandon your friends and make new ones.

2 You used to love maths but now you dread it. Quite often you don't understand what your teacher is talking about. Should you
a) Hide at the back of the classroom and hope she doesn't ask you any questions.
b) Tell her that you are struggling.
c) Ask a classmate to give you all the answers even though you don't understand them.

20

3 You never manage to finish all of your homework and are always getting into trouble at home and at school because of this. What can you do to improve things?

a) Make a homework schedule and stick to it. And make a point of doing your homework as soon as you come home from school.

b) Ask an older brother or sister to do it for you.

c) Continue to make up excuses (like your sister was practising her opera singing and you couldn't concentrate).

4 You've noticed that someone at school keeps throwing litter on the ground. Should you

a) Ask them to stop and explain that litter is dirty and can be harmful, especially to wildlife.

b) Ignore them.

c) Join in and drop your litter on the ground too.

5 You've been asked to read a poem in assembly. You hate reading out loud because you sometimes feel shy. Do you

a) Pretend to faint just before it is your turn to read.

b) Persuade your mum or dad that you can't go to school that day as you are really, really sick.

c) Practise reading your poem at home. Tell your teacher that you are feeling nervous but when the time comes, take a deep breath and do your best.

'Very dramatic, dear – you can star in the school play too!'

ANSWERS

1 a; 2 b; 3 a; 4 a; 5 c

21

The pirate and the princess

'Clementine O'Brian, where are you?' said Miss Ridley.
'Oh there you are! What are you doing hiding behind Sarah?
Clementine, you read so well yesterday that I would like you to
be Princess Roseanna. And Stephen Bryce, because you are
such a bundle of trouble, you will be the dastardly pirate
Captain Crank,' continued Miss Ridley. 'Paul Fisher you will be
the brave pirate Maximillian and Sarah you will be Princess
Roseanna's lady-in-waiting.'

The children in Year Five gathered around Miss Ridley laughing and cheering as they listened to her revelations about the play. All of them had something to do. If it wasn't in front of the lights, then it was backstage making props and scenes, doing make-up, costumes and hair. Everyone was involved.

The school play was going to be so much fun. Miss Ridley, the drama teacher, had written it herself. It was a story about a beautiful princess who was kidnapped by pirates and held to ransom. But her wicked stepfather, the King, decided that he valued his gold more than his stepdaughter. So Roseanna joined the pirates and together they attacked the wicked King's castle. The King was banished and Princess Roseanna and the brave pirate Maximillian became the much loved King and

Queen. What made the whole thing even more exciting was that all the pirates spoke in rap.

'Children, children,' shouted Miss Ridley above all the cheering and laughter, 'don't forget, the first rehearsal will be tomorrow in the hall, right after lunch. See you all then.'

And with that Miss Ridley was gone. It was almost as if she had disappeared in an enormous puff of smoke. She hadn't, of course, because Clementine could hear her shoes clip-clopping speedily down the corridor.

Clementine felt sick inside. The last thing she wanted to hear was that she had a leading role in the school play. She hated, in fact absolutely detested, being in front of an audience. She had wanted to do something backstage, maybe help make the props or paint the scenes. Anything but step out into the limelight and perform in front of other people. She would have to think of a way out of this situation.

The next day it rained. It rained and it rained and it rained. Playtime had been rained off, and so had PE, which would have included rounders, cricket and tennis. Instead Year Five had to make do with Mr Green's exercise routine in the gym.

Clementine couldn't concentrate on anything. She sat in the corner of the gym chewing her nails and staring out through the rain-splattered windows at the waterlogged sports field outside. She didn't even hear Mr Green, the PE teacher, call her name out when it was her turn to balance a book on her head and walk through an obstacle course.

IT'S A FACT

Isaac Newton, the famous scientist who discovered gravity, really struggled with maths at school.

'Clementine O'Brian. Are you with us or against us?,' said Mr Green. He always said silly things like that. 'Or should I say – Princess Roseanna, would you be so kind as to step this way,' he continued. 'Your loyal subjects are waiting for you to demonstrate your gracefulness and agility. So get moving!' And with that Mr Green shoved a book into her hands and pointed firmly to the beginning of the obstacle course.

Clementine, her face red from blushing, put the book on her head and walked nervously but successfully around Mr Green's tricky course. When she had finished the class clapped and Mr Green bowed. Clementine felt herself blush again. She just could not believe that Mr Green had already heard about her starring role. She was going to have to come up with a plan, and fast.

Right after lunch, Year Five made their way to the main hall where Miss Ridley was waiting for them. Her face beamed as they sat down on the floor in front of her. 'Girls and boys, this is going to be amazing! I've got your scripts,' she said eagerly. 'The sooner you learn your lines the better.'

IT'S A FACT
Walt Disney found school work hard. His teachers described him as slow and uncreative. As a young man, a newspaper fired him from his job as a cartoonist because he did not have any good ideas.

Clementine glanced around quickly at her classmates. They all seemed to be as cheerful and excited as Miss Ridley was. Clementine's hands shook as she grabbed a bunch of papers from Miss Ridley's outstretched arms. Then she quickly skimmed through the pages, anxiously counting Princess Roseanna's lines. It was just as she suspected – there were loads of them. Clementine felt her stomach go all queasy. Her mouth became dry, and she felt as if she simply could not speak. This was her worst nightmare.

26

'Right,' said Miss Ridley. 'Let's begin by reading the play together.

If there are any questions about your parts, don't call out, just put your hands up. I'll explain things as we go along. For those of you who don't have speaking roles, you are our audience. But, as you are listening to the play, I want you to think about the kinds of props, scenes and costumes you would like to make. You can jot down ideas on your scripts if you wish.

Okay, Stephen, as Captain Crank, you begin.'

Stephen Bryce looked at Miss Ridley and smiled. Then he began to read.

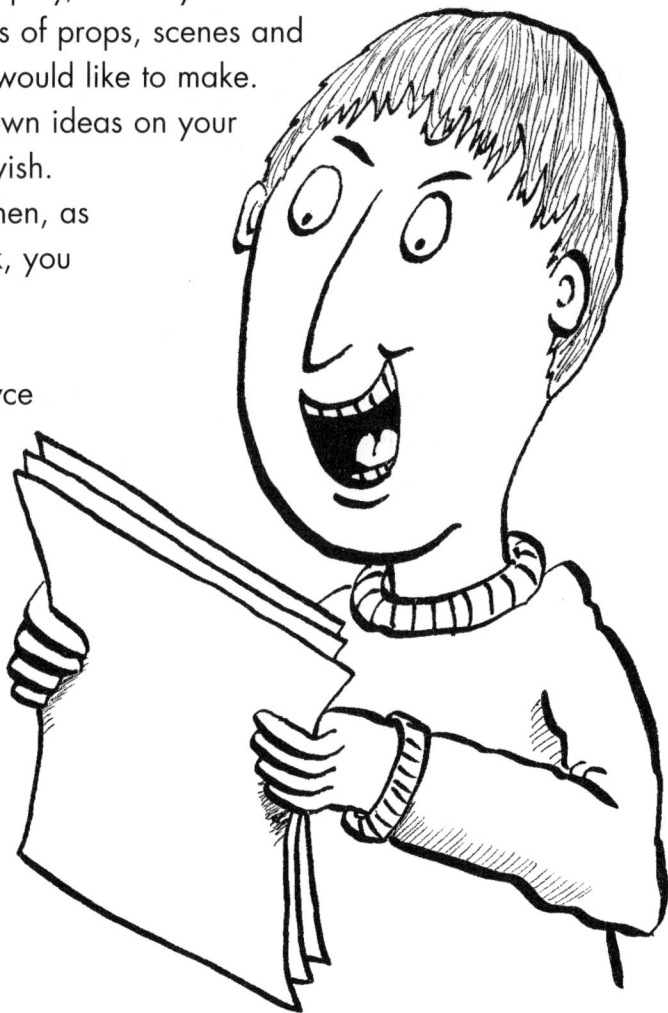

IT'S A FACT
Thomas Edison was an amazing inventor. However, he did so badly at school that he was asked to leave and his mother had to teach him at home.

'Welcome landlubbers, I'm glad you are here
To listen to my tale of kidnap and fear.
The story begins, oh, a long time ago,
When pirates were dastardly and everyone's foe.
One pirate, named Crank, that's me I confess
Stole a fair princess in a beautiful dress.
I demanded gold coins for her speedy return,
But her father was naught but a slippery worm.
For his daughter he cared not, but his gold quite a lot,
So he told me to keep her, he cared not a jot.
When Roseanna the princess heard of this deed,
She decided to punish the King for his greed.
She dressed like a pirate and became my first mate,
Then led my boys through the castle gate.
The King was defeated and Roseanna went home.
But this time she was no longer alone.
For brave pirate Max, her heart he had won
And together they ruled their kingdom as one.'

Stephen had rapped his
opening lines with incredible
confidence. When he had
finished, the class clapped
loudly and Stephen smiled
broadly.

'Well done, Stephen.
I can see that you are going
to make an excellent
Captain Crank,' said
Miss Ridley.

Clementine could feel
her heart pounding.
It was her turn to read
next. In a blind panic, she
put her hand up.

'Yes, Clementine. You're
next,' said a happy Miss Ridley.

'It's not that, Miss. I need
to go to the bathroom,' said
Clementine in a shaky voice.

'What, now?' asked a slightly agitated Miss Ridley.
'Can't you wait?'

'No, Miss, I need to go now,' insisted Clementine.

'Oh well, I'll get someone else to
read your lines while you are gone.
But hurry up,' sighed Miss Ridley.

Clementine dashed towards the
hall door. As she opened it, she
heard her friend Sarah reading
her opening lines. As soon as she
was out of the hall, she walked as
slowly as she could towards the
girls' toilets. She knew that if she
really took her time, she might not
have to read anything – at least
for now.

IT'S A FACT
John F. Kennedy
became one of the
most successful
American
presidents.
Throughout his
life he struggled
with a learning
difficulty called
dyslexia.

Clementine's plan worked. When she returned to the hall, she could tell that Miss Ridley had just begun talking about the play's main battle scene.

Miss Ridley's eager pirates had wanted to know how this incredibly dramatic scene was going be staged. Then, when Miss Ridley had finished explaining, those involved in prop- and scene-making were keen to tell her about their ideas.

Finally, it was time to go back to their classroom.

As Clementine walked along the corridor with her friend Sarah, she began to relax. Her heart was no longer pounding and the knot in her stomach did not feel quite so bad. She felt relieved but she knew that the problem had not gone away.

Just then Stephen Bryce patted her on the back.

IT'S A FACT
Michael Jordan, one of basketball's most brilliant players, did not get on to his school basketball team because his coach thought that he wasn't good enough.

'Too bad. You missed your lines,' said Stephen. 'You missed the bit when I kidnapped you and took you to my pirate ship. Then I locked you in the hold and left you there in the dark with all the mice and rats nibbling your toes!' continued Stephen enthusiastically.

'Oh well, I'm sure you had fun,' said Clementine, trying to hide her relief.

'Yeah, it was cool,' replied Stephen as he nudged past Clementine, now eager to join his huddle of friends just in front of him.

'See yuh,' and with that he was gone, racing ahead with his fellow pirates, all trying to be the first one to reach the classroom door.

That evening Clementine was unusually quiet. At teatime she hardly spoke, even when her younger brother Chris wanted to chat to her about his favourite subjects – monsters, aliens and ghosts. Her mum thought she was ill, and her dad checked her temperature. Clementine reassured them that she was simply feeling tired and that she felt like an early night. And for the rest of the evening she stayed in her room.

Later, when everyone was asleep, Clementine lay awake, staring at the shadows her night-light cast upon the ceiling. She was trying to figure out why she felt so uncomfortable speaking in front of other people.

Clementine could think of only one reason why she felt the way she did. It was just the way she was, it was part of her personality and she didn't know how to change it.

31

The next morning Clementine's mum dropped her off at Sarah's house because the girls had decided to walk to school together. As usual Sarah was bubbling over with enthusiasm about the day ahead. However she couldn't help noticing that Clementine seemed more than a little glum.

'Are you okay, Clem? Have I done something to upset you?' asked a concerned Sarah as they walked along the tree-lined streets together.

'No,' was all Clementine could bring herself to say.

'Has someone else upset you then?' persisted Sarah.

'No, it's just!', and with that Clementine burst into tears.

And so as the girls made their way to school, Clementine began to explain the reason why she felt so awful. When she had finished speaking, Sarah turned to Clementine and put an arm around her shoulders.

'It's okay to be shy. Not everyone's like me, you know, always wanting to be the centre of attention. All you have to do, Clem, is tell Miss Ridley how you are feeling. She'll understand. And she certainly won't want you to be miserable. Go and talk to her first thing this morning. But I have to say that I think it's a shame. You did read Princess Roseanna's part better than anyone else – even me!' laughed Sarah, as she gently nudged Clementine.

Clementine felt better all ready. She had finally managed to put into words how she had been feeling. And Sarah, who was super confident, didn't seem to think that she was weird because of how she felt.

As the girls strolled into the school playground, they spotted Miss Ridley parking her car.

'Go on,' urged Sarah. 'Tell her you need to speak to her and that it's important. And while you're at it tell her that I would love to be Princess Roseanna,' said Sarah with a broad grin on her face.

Clementine returned the smile and then raced off to catch Miss Ridley before she disappeared into the staff room.

Miss Ridley was just checking that she had unloaded all the necessary books, homework, projects and papers from her car when Clementine appeared at her side.

'Good morning, Clementine,' said Miss Ridley from behind her carefully constructed pile of classwork. 'You're bright and early this morning.'

'Yes, Miss. Um, I need to, um... I want to tell you, er ...,' stuttered Clementine as she struggled to find the right words.

'Is there a problem Clementine? If there is, just tell me,' replied Miss Ridley with a concerned look upon her face. 'I know, let's go to my classroom, then we can sit down quietly and you can tell me what's wrong. And, you can help me carry some of this stuff,' smiled Miss Ridley as she handed mountains of paper over to Clementine.

Five minutes later Clementine was seated at a desk with Miss Ridley beside her.

'Now Clementine, tell me all about it. And, whatever the problem is, I'm sure it can be sorted out,' said Miss Ridley in a gentle voice.

'I don't want to be Princess Roseanna,' blurted out Clementine. 'I hate it when everyone's looking at me. It makes me feel really nervous. My face turns bright red and I can't speak. I'll just be rubbish. You need someone who's better at that kind of thing. Please, Miss, don't make me do it.'

Miss Ridley remained silent for several moments after Clementine had finished speaking. She simply stared at Clementine's miserable face. Then, having gathered her thoughts together, she reached out and gently patted Clementine's clenched fists.

'I see,' began Miss Ridley. 'Well the solution is quite simple – we get someone else to play the part of Princess Roseanna.'

'Sarah would love to,' exclaimed Clementine as she tried her hardest not to burst into tears. She felt so relieved. In fact, she felt as if the biggest burden in the world had just been lifted from her shoulders.

'Yes, that might work,' replied Miss Ridley. 'But before I decide who is going to take your place, there are one or two things I want to say to you.

First, when I asked you to read the other day, you weren't expecting it and so you read beautifully. In fact, you were one of the best. The reason, I suspect, is that you hadn't had a chance to worry or get yourself in a state beforehand. Second, I think you really do have a natural talent. And there are ways to overcome shyness. Most people feel shy at times. But we won't start with a leading role in the school play. However, I would really like you to take a very small speaking part instead. I'll make sure that it's just one or two lines. If you do this, it really will help you to feel more confident. And, I bet it will help you to see that it's not as difficult as you think. Will you do this for me?'

'Okay, I'll do it,' she whispered. 'I'll try my best anyway.'

'Deal,' said Miss Ridley. 'Now off you go to your classroom. Oh and by the way, tell Sarah she's got the part if she wants it.'

The next four weeks of school passed by in a flash. For Year Five, every spare moment seemed to be taken up with rehearsing, making props and scenery and everyone getting more and more excited. Sarah turned out to be a fantastic princess. She even managed to get a few extra lines added to the script. And Clementine, who was now a pirate, didn't hate having to say, 'Stand back or I'll pickle your eyeballs!' In fact, at times, she quite enjoyed it as her line always got a laugh.

Finally, the big night came. As Clementine put her eye patch on, she peeped out from behind the stage curtain. Gathered around her were many of her classmates dressed in the most fantastic costumes.

'Are there many people out there?' asked Sarah anxiously.

'The hall is absolutely packed full of people,' whispered Clementine.

And it was. All the tickets had been sold and the hall was crammed full of eager parents, grandparents, brothers, sisters and, of course, teachers.

The play began with Captain Crank's dramatic entrance, followed by loud cheers and boos from the audience. When the time came for Clementine to make her appearance, Miss Ridley came to stand next to her. Clementine tried hard to ignore the butterflies in her stomach.

'Good luck,' smiled Miss Ridley.

'Thanks.' said Clementine.

And with that Clementine jumped on to the stage with a flourish. Seconds later the audience erupted into laughter. Clementine had delivered her line brilliantly. And suddenly she found herself wishing she had one or two more!

POWERFUL PEOPLE

Here are a couple of powerful people to inspire you. Maybe you can think of more people who have overcome difficulties in their lives and have achieved great things.

HARRIET TUBMAN
1820–1913

Harriet was born in Maryland, USA, in 1820. She was the daughter of slaves and she herself became a slave on a plantation. Harriet was first sent to work when she was five years old. Most slaves were treated badly and were often beaten. This happened to Harriet. Eventually Harriet ran away. She escaped by hiking through swamps and woods for over 60 kilometres. Harriet got a job and made a new life for herself. But she could not forget about her family and friends, and so she went back to rescue them. In all, Harriet made 19 rescue trips, helping slaves to escape from cruel slave masters. Harriet knew that slavery was unjust and inhuman and so she devoted her life to helping slaves. Queen Victoria heard about her work, and in 1893 she awarded Harriet a silver medal.

'I've got it!'

$$E = MC^2$$

ALBERT EINSTEIN
1879–1955

Albert Einstein did not speak until he was four years old and
didn't read until he was seven. His teachers said he was slow,
unfriendly and a day-dreamer. But as Albert became older, he
grew more and more curious about the world in which we live.
He developed interests in all kinds of things, such as science,
nature and space. And he became hardworking and patient.
If it took him 20 attempts to get something right, then
he just kept on trying until he succeeded.

Although not a success at school, Albert
became interested in one subject in particular
– maths. His ability in maths enabled
him to explore and figure out
things about our universe and
how it works. Albert's scientific
discoveries and theories –
such as his theory of relativity
– changed science and our
world forever. In 1921, he
received the Nobel Prize.

THAT'S ASTONISHING!

⭐ **SLOW STARTER**
Winston Churchill was
not a star at school. His school
reports show that he had trouble
with almost every subject.
However, he went on to become
Prime Minister of Britain and lead
his country during the Second
World War.

⭐ **A GREAT WOMAN**
The author Louisa May Alcott
was advised by her family to find
work as a servant or a seamstress.
And an editor told her she would
never write anything worthwhile.
She went on to write *Little Women*,
an extremely successful book.

⭐ **BAD STUDENT**
Louis Pasteur developed vaccination against infectious
diseases and pasteurization. But he was a very average student.
One year in chemistry, he came 15th out of 22 in his class.

★ Football Legend

Pelé is thought to be one of the greatest football players who ever lived. He was born in Brazil and as a boy was very poor. He shined shoes until he was 11 years old to help his family. Then his talents were discovered. Pelé went on to play for a top Brazilian team and his country. Between 1956 and 1974, Pelé scored a total of 1220 goals. While he played, Brazil won the World Cup three times.

★ Special Talent

Helen Keller was less than two years old when she became ill with a fever. Her illness left her blind and deaf. But, with the help of a special teacher, she overcame her disabilities, and as an adult she appeared on stage, telling audiences about her experiences. She devoted her life to making others aware that people with disabilities have a great deal to offer and that they should not be treated differently.

★ Perfect President

During his career, Abraham Lincoln lost an election campaign because he did not support slavery but went on to become president of the United States in 1860. As president, he helped to bring about the end of slavery in the USA.

★ INSPIRATIONAL LEADER

Gandhi was an Indian Nationalist leader who believed in achieving India's independence through peaceful actions. He was opposed to violence. Whenever fighting broke out during the Indian struggle for independence from Britain, Gandhi fasted to show how strongly he felt.

★ WOMEN'S RIGHTS

Susan B. Anthony devoted her life to women's rights. Her first job was as a teacher. At that time, women were paid less than men for the same job. Susan protested and lost her job. She helped to establish the National Woman Suffrage Association. In 1872, she tried to vote in a general election in the United States but was arrested. Fourteen years after her death in 1906, women in the US were finally allowed to vote.

THINGS TO DO

Dear Reader

Here are some ideas of things to do that will make you think about how you fit into the world. You could team up with a friend and compare your ideas.

1 Write down the top ten things that make you most proud of being you.

2 Draw or paint a self-portrait.

3 Get together with your friends and ask each one to make a list of the five people they most admire. (You do one as well.) Then compare with each other the people you have chosen. Ask each person why they chose the people they did.

4 Write a budget plan to help you manage your money better. If you get pocket money, write a weekly plan which should include all the things you buy, like comics and sweets. Try to find a way to save up a little. (For example, perhaps you only need two packets of sweets and not three!)

5 Make a homework plan or schedule. Figure out how long it usually takes you to work on each homework subject. Try to do your homework as soon as you come home from school. If you are organized and get your homework done, you will have lots of time left over for all those other things you love to do.

6 If you are concerned about the environment, there are a number of simple steps you and your friends can take to help out. You can encourage everyone you know to:
• Recycle household waste.
• Walk instead of driving when they go shopping.
• Use public transport, such as buses and trains, whenever possible.
• Save water, by taking showers instead of baths and not keeping the tap running when they brush their teeth.
• Get involved in a local environmental project.

7 Watch out for bullying. If you discover that someone is being bullied, tell an adult.

8 Join an after-school club. Choose something that you feel sure you will enjoy. This is a great way to make new friends.

ASKING FOR HELP

If you need help or advice about all kinds of things there are lots of organizations or agencies you can contact. Here are just a few:

Childline, 2nd Floor, Royal Mail Building, Studd Street, London N1 0QW
Freephone 0800 1111

Careline, Cardinal Heenan Centre, 326 High Road, Ilford, IG1 1QP
Phone 020 8514 5444

Survivors UK at: www.survivorsuk.co.uk
Offers support for those who have experienced abuse.

Teen Advice Online at: www.teenadviceonline.org

Kidscape, 2 Grosvenor Gardens, London SW1W ODH
Phone 020 7730 3300
Kidscape deals with abuse issues.

National Association for Special Education Needs,
NASEN House, 4–5 Amber Business Village,
Amber Close, Amington, Tamworth,
Staffordshire B77 4RP
Phone 01827 311500

National Council for One-Parent Families,
255 Kentish Town Road, London NW5 2LX
Phone 020 7428 5400

Anti-Bullying Campaign, 185 Tower Bridge Road, London SE1 2UF
Send SAE
Phone 020 7378 1446 or 020 7378 1447 or 020 7378 1448
or 020 7378 1449

Fleet Financial Group at www.fleetkids.com provide lots of info on saving and budgeting.

YoungBiz.com at www.youngbiz.com can give you advice on setting up businesses and investing your money.

GLOSSARY

ABILITY The skill or talent to do a particular thing.

ACHIEVEMENT A plan or aim that has been carried out.

ACTIVITY A thing to do.

AMBITION A strong desire to achieve a particular goal.

ATTITUDE A certain way of thinking or acting.

CHALLENGE Something that needs effort or hard work.

CONFIDENCE A strong belief in one's abilities.

DOUBT To feel unsure.

EDUCATION Knowledge received through some form of schooling.

EFFORT Trying hard to achieve something.

GOAL An aim or end result that someone tries to reach.

HOBBY Something someone likes to do for pleasure in their spare time.

BUDGET A plan to help you manage money.

CAREER A job, occupation or profession.

PRIDE The feeling of self-belief and self-worth.

PROBLEM Something that seems difficult or an obstacle.

QUALIFICATION A skill or special training that makes a person fit for a particular job or activity.

IDENTIFY To recognize or figure out.

INTEREST Money paid to you by a bank or building society for saving your money with them. Also means a hobby or something you are interested in.

ISSUE A point of particular interest or concern.

SKILL An ability to do something well.

SOLUTION The answer to a problem; the way to solve a problem.

SUCCESS A desired result.

TALENT A special ability.

POLLUTION Harmful substances that affect the environment.

VIEW A way of looking at a situation; an opinion.

INDEX